A GIFT FOR:

My best friend, my soooouull Twin!

FROM:

Joni

DATE:

November 21, 2005

Crazy About My Friend

BARBOUR
PUBLISHING

CRAZY ABOUT MY FRIEND™

COPYRIGHT © 2003 BY MARK GILROY COMMUNICATIONS, INC.
TULSA, OKLAHOMA

ART AND DESIGN BY JACKSONDESIGNCO,LLC
SILOAM SPRINGS, ARKANSAS

ISBN 1-59310-427-8

ALL RIGHTS RESERVED. NO PART OF THIS PUBLICATION MAY
BE REPRODUCED OR TRANSMITTED IN ANY FORM OR BY ANY MEANS
WITHOUT WRITTEN PERMISSION OF THE PUBLISHER.

Scripture quotations marked NLT are taken from the Holy Bible, New Living
Translation, copyright © 1996. Used by permission of Tyndale House Publishers, Inc.
Wheaton, Illinois 60189, U.S.A. All rights reserved.

Scripture quotations marked NKJV are taken from the New King James Version. Copyright ©
1979, 1980, 1982, by Thomas Nelson, Inc. Used by permission. All rights reserved.

PUBLISHED BY BARBOUR PUBLISHING, INC., P.O. BOX 719,
UHRICHSVILLE, OHIO 44683, www.barbourpublishing.com

Member of the
Evangelical Christian
Publishers Association

PRINTED IN CHINA.

You Are Loved

"I MYSELF HAVE GAINED MUCH JOY
AND COMFORT FROM YOUR LOVE."

PHILEMON 1:7 NLT

"A FRIEND LOVES AT ALL TIMES."

PROVERBS 17:17 NKJV

I'M CRAZY ABOUT MY FRIEND
BECAUSE SHE STICKS BY ME
THROUGH THICK AND THIN.

I'M CRAZY ABOUT MY FRIEND
BECAUSE SHE LOVES A SALE
ALMOST AS MUCH AS I DO.

I'M CRAZY ABOUT MY FRIEND
BECAUSE SHE KNOWS
HOW TO MAKE ME LAUGH.

I'M CRAZY ABOUT MY FRIEND
BECAUSE TOGETHER WE LOOK COOL.

I'M CRAZY ABOUT MY FRIEND BECAUSE SHE AGREES WITH ME THAT CHOCOLATE-CHIMPANZEE-MARSHMALLOW-NUTTY-HEAVEN ICE CREAM IS ACTUALLY A FIFTH FOOD GROUP.

.

I'M CRAZY ABOUT MY FRIEND
BECAUSE SHE HAS A WONDERFUL
SENSE OF FASHION.

I'M CRAZY ABOUT MY FRIEND
BECAUSE SHE ACCEPTS ME
JUST THE WAY I AM.

I'M CRAZY ABOUT MY FRIEND
BECAUSE SHE IS UP ON ALL
THE LATEST BEAUTY TREATMENTS.

I'M CRAZY ABOUT MY FRIEND
BECAUSE SHE HELPS ME STAY
UP-TO-DATE ON CURRENT EVENTS.

Oh my! And then what did she say?

"Ain't no stopping us now..."

I'M CRAZY ABOUT MY FRIEND
BECAUSE EVEN AS WE GET
A LITTLE OLDER, THE TWO OF US
STILL REALLY KNOW HOW TO ROCK!

I'M CRAZY ABOUT MY FRIEND
BECAUSE SHE DOESN'T SWEAT
THE SMALL STUFF IN LIFE.

I'M CRAZY ABOUT MY FRIEND
BECAUSE EVEN THOUGH
WE HAVE OUR DIFFERENCES,
WE STILL LOVE EACH OTHER.

I'M CRAZY ABOUT MY FRIEND BECAUSE
SHE IS AN INCREDIBLE MULTITASKER.

I'M CRAZY ABOUT MY FRIEND
BECAUSE SHE IS ALWAYS
THE PERFECT HOSTESS.

I'M CRAZY ABOUT MY FRIEND
BECAUSE SHE KNOWS HOW
TO CHEER ME UP WHEN I'M BLUE.

I'M CRAZY ABOUT MY FRIEND
BECAUSE SHE ISN'T AFRAID
OF A LITTLE HARD WORK.

I'M CRAZY ABOUT MY FRIEND
BECAUSE SHE UNDERSTANDS
WHAT MAKES A GREAT MOVIE.

I'M CRAZY ABOUT MY FRIEND
BECAUSE SHE KNOWS
THERE'S A TIME TO SLOW DOWN
AND ENJOY GOD'S CREATION.

I'M CRAZY ABOUT MY FRIEND
BECAUSE OF HER OUTRAGEOUS
SENSE OF ADVENTURE.

I'M CRAZY ABOUT MY FRIEND
BECAUSE SHE NEVER LETS SOMETHING
LIKE A BAD HAIR DAY GET HER DOWN.

I'M CRAZY ABOUT MY FRIEND BECAUSE
SHE HAS AN INCREDIBLE SPIRIT
OF PERSEVERANCE.

I'M CRAZY ABOUT MY FRIEND
BECAUSE SHE IS AS DEDICATED
TO FITNESS AS I AM.

I'M CRAZY ABOUT MY FRIEND BECAUSE
SHE CREATED THE PERFECT RECIPE
FOR CALORIE-FREE BIRTHDAY CAKE

(AND ICE CREAM).

I'M CRAZY ABOUT MY FRIEND
BECAUSE SHE KNOWS HOW
TO BRIGHTEN A RAINY DAY.

I'M CRAZY ABOUT MY FRIEND
BECAUSE SHE AND I HAVE SHARED
SO MANY OF THE SAME EXPERIENCES.

I'M CRAZY ABOUT MY FRIEND BECAUSE
SHE ALWAYS UNDERSTANDS MY MOODS.

I'M CRAZY ABOUT MY FRIEND BECAUSE
SHE REALLY CAN READ MY MIND.

I'M CRAZY ABOUT MY FRIEND
BECAUSE SHE WATCHES MY BACK.

I'M CRAZY ABOUT MY FRIEND BECAUSE
SHE HAS SUCH AN UPLIFTING SPIRIT~
SHE KEEPS ME MOTIVATED.

I'M CRAZY ABOUT MY FRIEND BECAUSE
SHE IS ALWAYS THOUGHTFUL TO LET ME
KNOW SHE IS THINKING OF ME.

I'M CRAZY ABOUT MY FRIEND BECAUSE
I FEEL LIKE I'VE KNOWN HER FOREVER.

I'M CRAZY ABOUT MY FRIEND
BECAUSE SHE SEES PAST MY FAULTS
(AND LOVES ME ANYWAY).

I'M CRAZY ABOUT MY FRIEND
BECAUSE EVEN IF WE DON'T TALK
FOR A LONG TIME, WE NEVER
STRUGGLE TO GET RIGHT BACK
TO WHERE WE WERE BEFORE!

I'M CRAZY ABOUT MY FRIEND BECAUSE
SHE CHALLENGES ME TO BE MY BEST.

I'M CRAZY ABOUT MY FRIEND
BECAUSE SHE HAS A BEAUTIFUL WAY
WITH WORDS AND KNOWS HOW
TO MAKE ME FEEL WONDERFUL.

I'M CRAZY ABOUT MY FRIEND
BECAUSE SHE HAS MASTERED
THE FINE ART OF SHARING.

I'M CRAZY ABOUT MY FRIEND
BECAUSE WE SHARE THE SAME VALUES
OF WHAT REALLY MATTERS IN LIFE.

I'M CRAZY ABOUT MY FRIEND
BECAUSE SHE IS SOMEONE I CAN TRUST
WITH ANYTHING GOING ON IN MY LIFE.

I'M CRAZY ABOUT MY FRIEND
BECAUSE SOME DAYS I'M POSITIVE
THAT GOD SENT HER AS AN ANGEL
TO BLESS MY LIFE.

I'M CRAZY ABOUT MY FRIEND BECAUSE
SHE IS ALWAYS THERE FOR ME~
EVEN WHEN SHE ISN'T PRESENT.

I'M CRAZY ABOUT MY FRIEND BECAUSE
SHE HAS A FORGIVING SPIRIT.

I'M CRAZY ABOUT MY FRIEND BECAUSE
SHE KNOWS EXACTLY THE RIGHT THING
TO SAY WHEN I NEED CHEERING UP.

I'M CRAZY ABOUT MY FRIEND
BECAUSE I NEED SOMEONE
WHO LOVES ME ENOUGH
TO PRAY FOR ME.

I'M CRAZY ABOUT MY FRIEND
BECAUSE SHE IS GOOD ABOUT
VISITING HER FATHER'S HOUSE.

I'M CRAZY ABOUT MY FRIEND
BECAUSE EVEN WHEN WE GET OLD
AND WRINKLED ~ WE WILL
STILL BE FRIENDS.

I'M CRAZY ABOUT MY FRIEND BECAUSE TRUE FRIENDS ARE FRIENDS FOREVER!

"EVERY TIME
I THINK OF YOU,
I GIVE THANKS
TO MY GOD."

PHILIPPIANS 1:3 NLT